TEAM SPIRIT ®

SMART BOOKS FOR YOUNG FANS

THE VANCOUVER CANUCKS

BY
MARK STEWART

CONTENT CONSULTANT
DENIS GIBBONS
SOCIETY FOR INTERNATIONAL HOCKEY RESEARCH

NORWOOD HOUSE PRESS
CHICAGO, ILLINOIS

Norwood House Press
P.O. Box 316598
Chicago, Illinois 60631

For information regarding Norwood House Press, please visit our website at:
www.norwoodhousepress.com or call 866-565-2900.

All photos courtesy of Associated Press except the following:
Hockey Hall of Fame (6, 8, 10, 16, 17, 29, 35 top, 41), Vancouver Canucks (7, 33),
Topps, Inc. (9, 15, 21, 31, 34 both, 45), O-Pee-Chee Ltd. (18), National Hockey League (22),
London Publishing Co. (27), Author's Collection (28, 37, 39, 43), Quarton Group/NHL (38),
The Upper Deck Co. (40, 42 both, 43 top).
Cover Photo: AP Photo/Ross D. Franklin

The memorabilia and artifacts pictured in this book are presented for educational and informational purposes,
and come from the collection of the author.

Editor: Mike Kennedy
Designer: Ron Jaffe
Project Management: Black Book Partners, LLC.
Special thanks to Topps, Inc.

Library of Congress Cataloging-in-Publication Data

Stewart, Mark, 1960 July 7-
 The Vancouver Canucks / by Mark Stewart.
  pages cm. -- (Team spirit)
 Includes bibliographical references and index.
 Summary: "A revised Team Spirit Hockey edition featuring the Vancouver Canucks that chronicles the history and accomplishments of the team. Includes access to the Team Spirit website which provides additional information and photos"-- Provided by publisher.
  ISBN 978-1-59953-628-6 (library edition : alk. paper) -- ISBN 978-1-60357-636-9 (ebook) 1. Vancouver Canucks (Hockey team)--History--Juvenile literature. I. Title.
 GV848.V36S74 2014
 796.962'640971133--dc23
                                                    2013030196

© 2014 by Norwood House Press.
Team Spirit® is a registered trademark of Norwood House Press.
All rights reserved.
No part of this book may be reproduced without written permission from the publisher.
•
The Vancouver Canucks is a registered trademark of Vancouver Canucks Limited Partnership.
This publication is not affiliated with Vancouver Canucks Limited Partnership,
The National Hockey League, or The National Hockey League Players Association.

239N—012014
Manufactured in the United States of America in Stevens Point, Wisconsin.

COVER PHOTO: The Canucks celebrate a goal during the 2012–13 season.

TABLE OF CONTENTS

CHAPTER	PAGE
MEET THE CANUCKS	4
GLORY DAYS	6
HOME ICE	12
DRESSED FOR SUCCESS	14
WE WON!	16
GO-TO GUYS	20
CALLING THE SHOTS	24
ONE GREAT DAY	26
LEGEND HAS IT	28
IT REALLY HAPPENED	30
TEAM SPIRIT	32
TIMELINE	34
FUN FACTS	36
TALKING HOCKEY	38
GREAT DEBATES	40
FOR THE RECORD	42
PINPOINTS	44
GLOSSARY	46
LINE CHANGE	47
INDEX	48

ABOUT OUR GLOSSARY

In this book, there may be several words that you are reading for the first time. Some are sports words, some are new vocabulary words, and some are familiar words that are used in an unusual way. All of these words are defined on page 46. Throughout the book, sports words appear in **bold type**. Regular vocabulary words appear in ***bold italic type***.

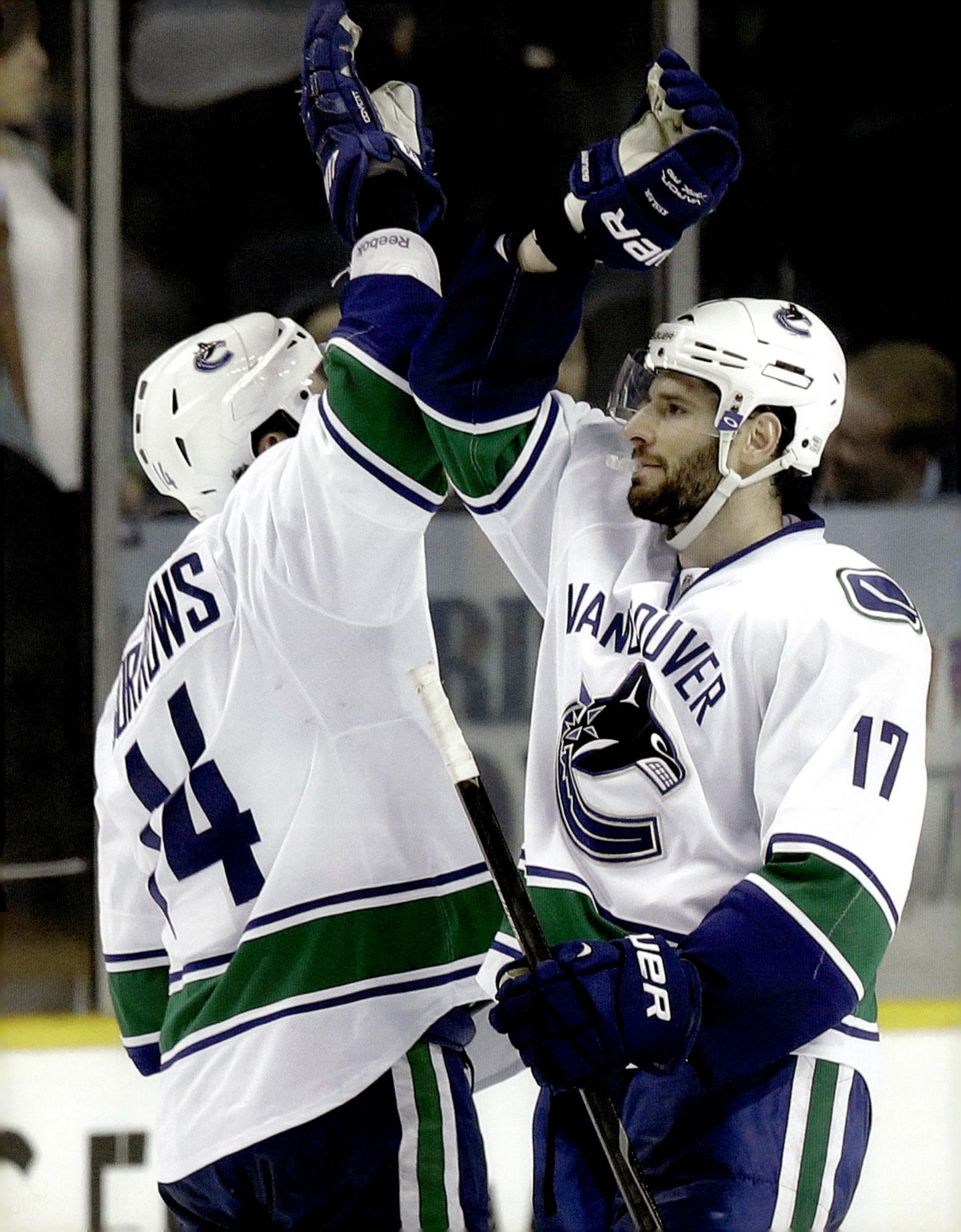
Reebok
17

MEET THE CANUCKS

Vancouver is one of the most relaxed and *diverse* cities in all of North America. It has a pleasant climate, and when the weekend arrives, there are lots of cool things to do and places to go. Walking down the streets of the city and its suburbs, it is easy to forget that it is home to one of Canada's seven **National Hockey League (NHL)** teams, the Canucks.

Year in and year out, the Canucks fill their lineup with talented stars and play exciting hockey. Their fans are more than loyal. They identify with the players and embrace them like family members. Every Vancouver fan has a favorite Canuck—you can tell by the 20 or 30 different jerseys in the stands during games.

This book tells the story of the Canucks. They are a source of intense pride for the people of Vancouver. Every player who pulls on a Canucks sweater knows that the fans will always be behind the team.

Alex Burrows and Ryan Kesler exchange a forearm bump after a win during the 2012–13 season.

GLORY DAYS

The Canucks played their first NHL season in 1970–71. However, professional hockey already had a long and colorful history in the city. Vancouver is an important seaport with access to the Pacific Ocean. It is located in the Canadian **province** of British Columbia. In the early 1900s, there were a lot of jobs and a lot of young workers in the city. Often, they spent their free time playing hockey and watching it.

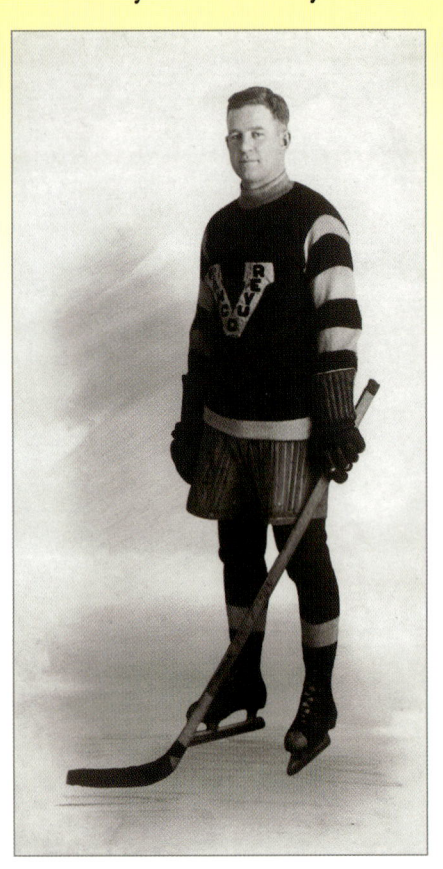

Vancouver had a team called the Millionaires. In 1915, they won the **Stanley Cup**. It marked the first time a club from the West Coast captured hockey's greatest prize. Over the years, the Millionaires featured some of Canada's top stars, including Fred "Cyclone" Taylor and Jack Adams.

As the NHL grew in size and power during the 1920s, western teams such as the Millionaires could no longer afford to pay the top players. West Coast hockey continued to thrive, but only for teams in the **minor leagues**. Vancouver was home to one of the most successful teams in the region at this level, the Canucks. They won six league championships from 1946 to 1970. Five players who skated for the Canucks during this time would later enter the **Hall of Fame**.

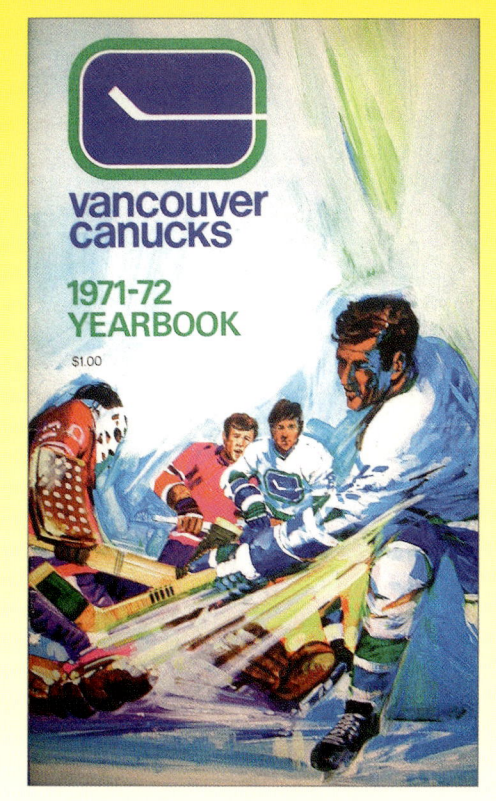

During the 1960s, the NHL decided to expand from six teams to 12. In 1970, the league grew to 14 teams with the addition of the Buffalo Sabres and the Canucks. At this point, Vancouver was a completely different team than the minor-league club. The new owners simply bought the old team so they could keep the name for the new one. They hired Bud Poile and coach Hall Laycoe to build a lineup from scratch. Poile had done the same job for the Philadelphia Flyers a few years earlier.

Vancouver and Buffalo were allowed to participate in a special **expansion draft**. The Canucks' first pick was Gary Doak,

LEFT: Jack Adams was one of Vancouver's first stars.
ABOVE: This yearbook was printed for the team's second season.

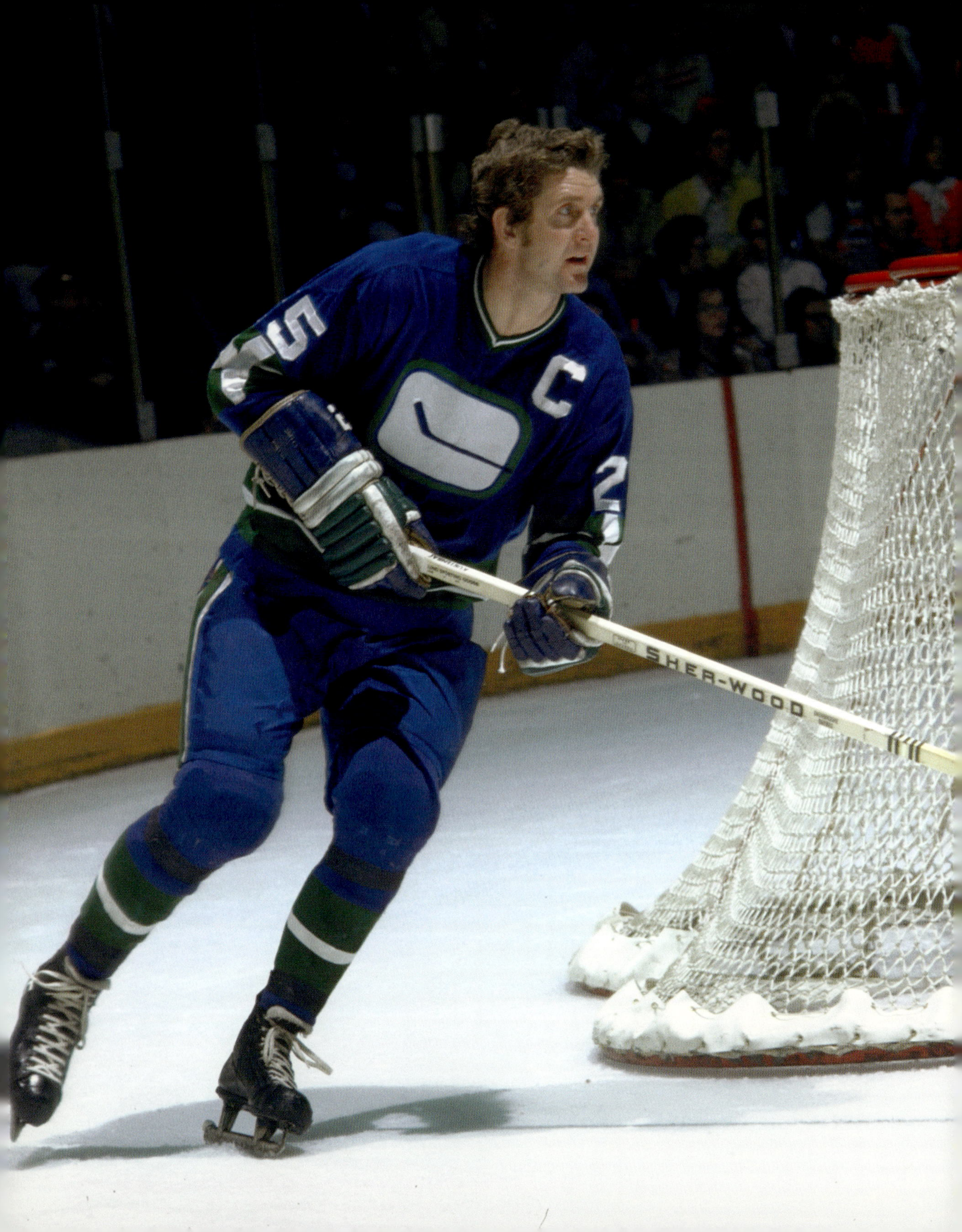
SHER-WOOD

a defenseman from the Boston Bruins. Next, the team took Orland Kurtenbach from the New York Rangers. Kurtenbach had played for the old Canucks in the 1950s when he was a teenager. He would become the team's first captain after it moved to the NHL. Another pick in this special draft was Pat Quinn of the Toronto Maple Leafs. Quinn would go on to coach the Canucks in the 1990s.

The Canucks had some talented players in the early 1970s, including Jocelyn Guevremont, Dale Tallon, Don Lever, and Andre Boudrias. However, they failed to make the **playoffs** in their first four seasons. Things began to look up in 1974–75. The Canucks finished with the best record in their **division** and their first winning record.

This season of promise was followed by 15 years of frustration. Try as they might, the Canucks simply could not find the winning formula, even though they had plenty of good players. Stan Smyl, Thomas Gradin, Patrik Sundstrom, and Tony Tanti ranked among the NHL's best scorers. Richard Brodeur was a quality goalie. But something always seemed to go wrong—except in 1981–82. That

LEFT: Orland Kurtenbach wore the captain's C for four seasons with the Canucks.
ABOVE: This trading card shows Pat Quinn during his playing days.

year, the Canucks got hot near the end of the season, made the playoffs, and whipped through the Western **Conference** to reach the **Stanley Cup Finals** for the first time. They lost to the New York Islanders.

In the 1990s, Quinn assembled one of the finest clubs in the NHL. Vancouver's top players were Pavel Bure, Trevor Linden, and Kirk McLean. Bure was nicknamed "The Russian Rocket." He had back-to-back 60-goal seasons before he turned 23. Linden became the team captain when he was 21. McLean, a goalie, joined Vancouver in the late-1980s and developed into a star. The Canucks won their division two years in a row. In 1993–94, Vancouver made it back to the Stanley Cup Finals. This time, they lost to another New York team, the Rangers, in a thrilling seven-game series.

From 2003–04 to 2012–13, the Canucks finished atop their division all but two times. The leaders of these teams included Markus Naslund, Mattias Ohlund, Todd Bertuzzi, Sami Salo, Roberto Luongo, Brendan Morrison, Ryan Kesler, Dan Hamhuis, and Alex Burrows. Naslund, Bertuzzi, and Morrison formed a high-scoring **line** called the "West Coast Express."

Vancouver's most popular players during this time were the Sedin twins, Henrik and Daniel. Henrik played center and Daniel played left wing. They brought the fans to their feet with excellent skating, passing, and shooting skills. The 2010–11 season was extra special for the Canucks and their fans. That spring, the team ripped through the Western Conference playoffs and reached the Stanley Cup Finals for the third time. Against each new opponent, a new star emerged—Burrows in one series, Kesler in another, and Henrik Sedin in another.

Vancouver fans were ready to start their long-awaited Stanley Cup party after the Canucks took a lead over the Boston Bruins in the finals. Unfortunately, the team lost its scoring touch in the last two games. Fans were upset about the missed opportunity, but they were proud of their players nonetheless. Their skill and unselfish play would serve as an example for future Canucks for a long time.

LEFT: Pavel Bure looks for a scoring opportunity.
ABOVE: Daniel Sedin, Dan Hamhuis, and Henrik Sedin are all smiles after a goal.

ROGERS ARENA
WELCOME TO THE STANLEY CUP FINAL
WELCOME TO THE STANLEY CUP FINAL
STANLEY CUP FINAL
ROGERS
SONY
HSBC
Coca-Cola zero
BEST BUY
RHINO

HOME ICE

The Canucks play in a modern arena located in downtown Vancouver. The building was completed in 1995, after the *National Basketball Association (NBA)* awarded a new team to Vancouver. Today, the Canucks are the city's only major-league sports team. Their home is named Rogers Arena, after a large Canadian *telecommunications* company.

Rogers Arena replaced the Canucks' first home, the Pacific Coliseum. The Pacific Coliseum was popular among NHL players because it had one of the best playing surfaces. The ice was thin and hard without being brittle. Thinner ice is closer to the cooling pipes underneath it, which makes for a smoother surface.

BY THE NUMBERS

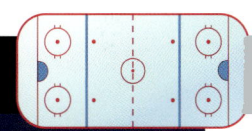

- The Canucks' arena has 18,910 seats for hockey.
- The LED scoreboard can display images in 4.4 trillion colors.
- As of 2013, the team has retired four numbers: 10 (Pavel Bure), 12 (Stan Smyl), 16 (Trevor Linden), and 19 (Markus Naslund). Numbers 11, 28, and 37 are not worn by Vancouver players in honor of three teammates who passed away.

The Canucks' arena is a great place for fans to enjoy a game.

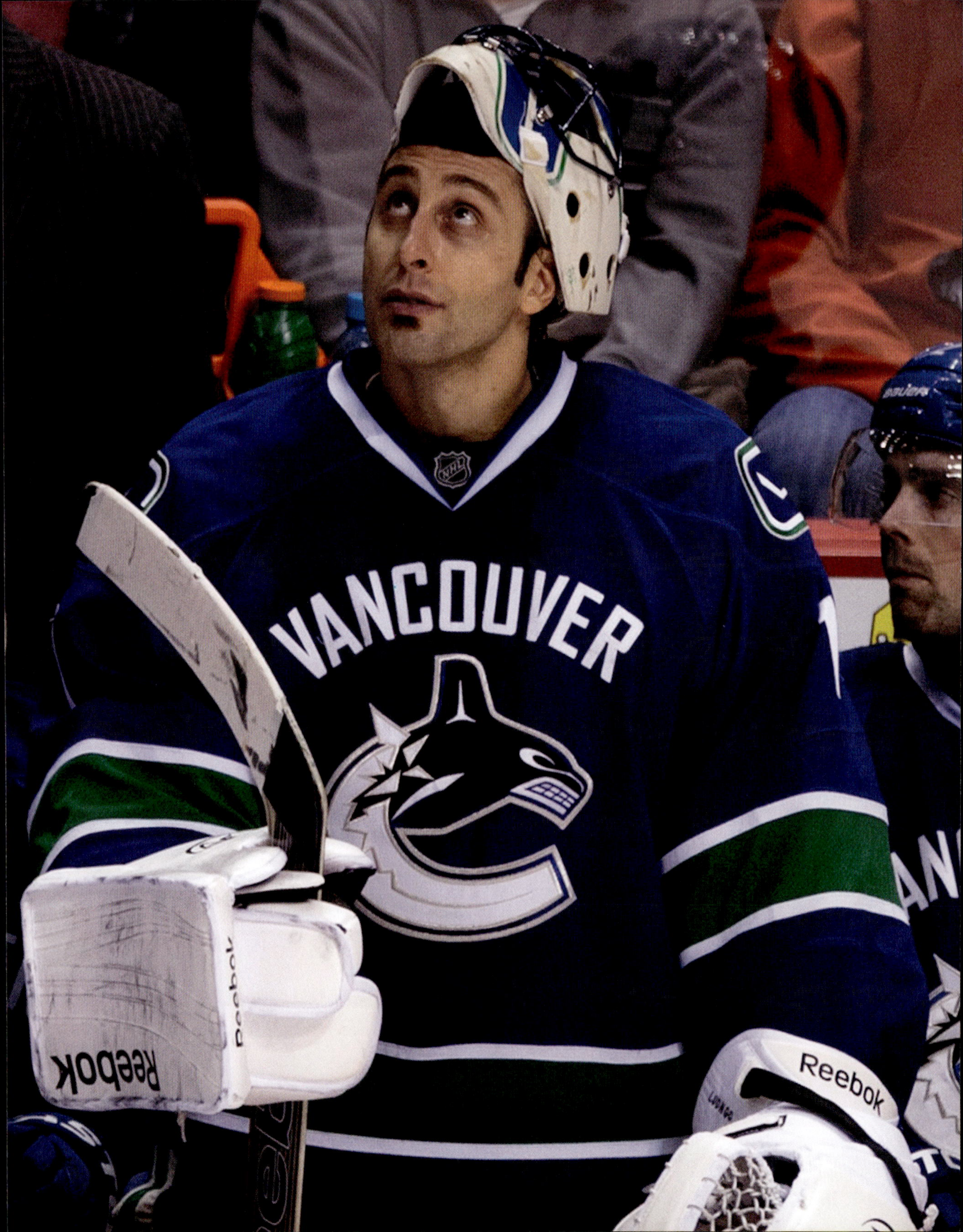
VANCOUVER
Reebok
Reebok
Reebok

DRESSED FOR SUCCESS

Canuck is a nickname for a Canadian. Where the word comes from is something of a mystery. Perhaps that is why the team's *logo* and uniform have changed so much over the years. Before the Canucks joined the NHL, their mascot was a lumberjack named Johnny Canuck.

In 1970, the Canucks wore green and blue jerseys. Their logo featured a hockey stick on the front against a background of a hockey rink. By the end of the 1970s, Vancouver had switched its logo and changed colors to yellow, orange, and black. In 1985, the Canucks used the team name on the jersey for the first time.

In 1997, the team made a dramatic change. The jersey showed a killer whale bursting through an ice sheet, with blue, red, and silver as the uniform colors. Over the next 15 years, more changes would come. Blue and green also returned as the team's colors.

LEFT: Robert Luongo wears Vancouver's home uniform during the 2012–13 season.
ABOVE: Andre Boudrias models the team's first uniform.

WE WON!

The Canucks made their first trip to the Stanley Cup Finals at the end of the 1981–82 season. Even though Vancouver finished with a losing record, the team got hot and went into the playoffs undefeated in their final nine games. The offensive heroes included Thomas Gradin, Curt Fraser, Ivan Boldirev, and Ivan Hlinka, who became the NHL's first Czech star. Harold Snepts, Tiger Williams, and goalie Richard Brodeur led the defense.

In five previous trips to the playoffs, the Canucks had yet to win a single series. This time, things were different. The popular and hard-working Stan Smyl had been named captain late in the year. Also, Roger Neilson was promoted to head coach in March, after Harry Neale was suspended by the league for getting into a shoving match with a fan.

LEFT: Stan Smyl and Harold Snepts celebrate the victory that got the Canucks into the 1982 Stanley Cup Finals.
RIGHT: Geoff Courtnall fires a slapshot.

It was as if the Canucks had hit the "reset" button when the **postseason** started. Vancouver defeated the Calgary Flames, Los Angeles Kings, and Chicago Blackhawks in the first three rounds of the playoffs. In all, the team lost just twice as it rolled toward a meeting in the Stanley Cup Finals with the New York Islanders. The Canucks nearly took Game 1, losing in **overtime**. The next three games were hard-fought, but the experienced Islanders outplayed the young Canucks and swept the series.

Vancouver's next visit to the championship round came in the spring of 1994. This club finished just one game over .500. But the Vancouver lineup featured some of hockey's most exciting players, including Trevor Linden, Pavel Bure, Geoff Courtnall, and Kirk McLean. Pat Quinn—a defenseman for the Canucks in the 1970s—coached the team.

In the opening round of the playoffs, Vancouver did the impossible. After falling behind to the Calgary Flames, the Canucks won three games in a row and took the series. Each victory ended with a heart-stopping overtime goal. In Game 7, after McLean made a remarkable save, Bure scored the winning goal on a great pass from Jeff Brown.

The Canucks now seemed unstoppable. They wiped out the Dallas Stars and Toronto Maple Leafs to reach the Stanley Cup Finals against the New York Rangers. Vancouver fans couldn't believe it when their team lost three of the first four games. The Canucks battled back to even the series. In Game 7, Linden—who was playing with broken ribs—scored two great goals, but Vancover came up just short by a score of 3–2.

Vancouver's third appearance in the Stanley Cup Finals came in 2010–11. The Canucks survived tough playoff series with the Blackhawks, Nashville Predators, and San Jose Sharks. The victory over Chicago was the sweetest. The Blackhawks were the defending NHL champs. They had knocked the Canucks out of the playoffs the previous two seasons. The series went seven nail-biting games. Game 7 was decided on a sliding save by Roberto Luongo, followed by an overtime goal by Alex Burrows. Henrik and Daniel Sedin led the club through the playoffs, with big contributions from Burrows, Luongo, Ryan Kesler, and Kevin Bieksa.

The Canucks faced the Boston Bruins in the Stanley Cup Finals and won the first two games at home. Boston tied the series, but the Canucks took Game 5 with a thrilling 1–0 victory. That win seemed to sap the strength of Vancouver's players. The Bruins won the final two games to deny the Canucks their long-awaited first Stanley Cup.

LEFT: Trevor Linden was the leader of the 1993–94 Canucks.
ABOVE: Roberto Luongo rushes to join the celebration after Vancouver's victory over the Chicago Blackhawks.

GO-TO GUYS

To be a true star in the NHL, you need more than a great slapshot. You have to be a "go-to guy"—someone teammates trust to make the winning play when the seconds are ticking away in a big game. Canucks fans have had a lot to cheer about over the years, including these great stars.

THE PIONEERS

ANDRE BOUDRIAS   Center

- BORN: 9/19/1943   • PLAYED FOR TEAM: 1970–71 TO 1975–76

Andre Boudrias was the top scorer on the Canucks in four of their first five seasons. He loved to challenge opponents when they had the puck and out-skate them when *he* had it. His nickname was "Super Pest."

ORLAND KURTENBACH   Center

- BORN: 9/7/1936   • PLAYED FOR TEAM: 1970–71 TO 1973–74

Orland Kurtenbach was known as a solid all-around player when he joined the Canucks. His shooting, passing, defense, and hard work inspired his teammates. Kurtenbach was a great leader for a young team.

THOMAS GRADIN   Center

- BORN: 2/18/1956
- PLAYED FOR TEAM: 1978–79 TO 1985–86

Thomas Gradin was already a major star in Europe when he decided to try his luck in the NHL. He led the Canucks in **assists** in five of his first six seasons. Gradin had 19 points (goals plus assists) in 17 playoff games during Vancouver's 1982 run to the Stanley Cup Finals.

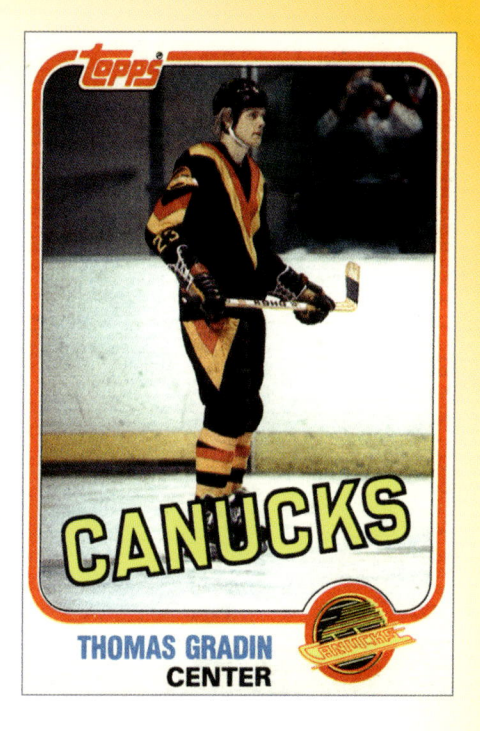

STAN SMYL   Right Wing/Left Wing

- BORN: 1/28/1958   • PLAYED FOR TEAM: 1978–79 TO 1990–91

Stan Smyl was known as "Steamer," and no one in the league skated harder than he did. Smyl was captain of the Canucks for eight seasons. He retired with the team records for goals, assists, and games played. Smyl's number 12 was the first uniform retired by the team.

PATRIK SUNDSTROM   Center

- BORN: 12/14/1961   • PLAYED FOR TEAM: 1982–83 TO 1986–87

There was very little Patrik Sundstrom could not do with a hockey stick in his hand. He was a swift skater, an accurate shooter, and a crafty passer. In his second season with Vancouver, Sundstrom set a team record for centers with 38 goals.

ABOVE: This trading card shows Thomas Gradin during a break in the action.

MODERN STARS

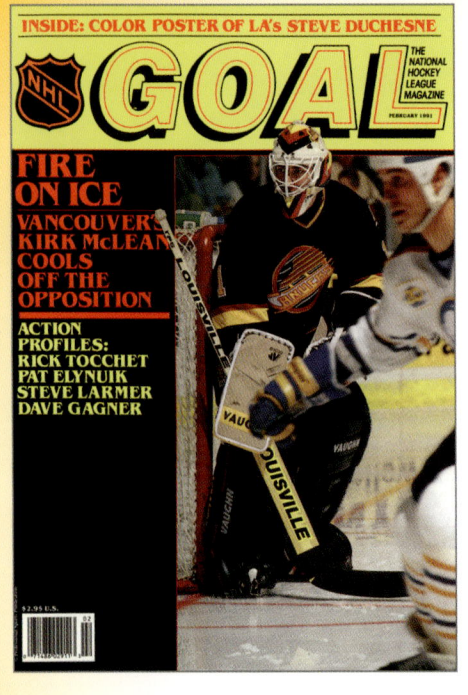

KIRK McLEAN — Goalie

- Born: 6/26/1966
- Played for Team: 1987–88 to 1997–98

Vancouver fans were nervous when the Canucks parted with Patrik Sundstrom to get Kirk McLean. But McLean led the team back to the Stanley Cup Finals in 1994. McLean's 1,544 minutes in goal during the playoffs that spring set a new record.

TREVOR LINDEN — Center/Right Wing

- Born: 4/11/1970
- Played for Team: 1988–89 to 1997–98 & 2001–02 to 2007–08

Trevor Linden's skill and leadership convinced the Canucks to make him their captain at the age of 21. Linden was a tough player with a great scoring touch. When Vancouver lost two centers in 1992–93, Linden agreed to switch to that position and led the team to its first 100-point season.

PAVEL BURE — Right Wing

- Born: 3/31/1971 • Played for Team: 1991–92 to 1997–98

Pavel Bure was the star of the Russian "Red Army" team before joining the Canucks. Despite suffering from sore knees most of his career, he was one of the league's fastest skaters and best scorers. The Russian Rocket had 254 goals in his career with Vancouver.

MARKUS NASLUND   Left Wing

- BORN: 7/30/1973   • PLAYED FOR TEAM: 1995–96 TO 2007–08

Markus Naslund had one of the best **wrist shots** in the history of the NHL. If a goalie blinked, the puck was already past him. Naslund led the Canucks in points seven years in a row.

HENRIK SEDIN   Center

- BORN: 9/26/1980   • FIRST SEASON WITH TEAM: 2000–01

Henrik Sedin was half of one of the best brother combinations in hockey history. Henrik was a superb passer and playmaker. He led the league in assists three years in a row.

DANIEL SEDIN   Left Wing

- BORN: 9/26/1980   • FIRST SEASON WITH TEAM: 2000–01

Having the Sedin brothers on the same line was like having two players who think as one. Daniel was an excellent goal-scorer who often benefitted from the hard work of his brother. His best season came in 2010–11 when he scored 41 goals and added 63 assists.

RYAN KESLER   Center

- BORN: 8/31/1984   • FIRST SEASON WITH TEAM: 2003–04

Ryan Kesler had a reputation as a superb defensive center in his early years with the Canucks. He worked hard to improve the rest of his game and eventually played in the **All-Star Game**. In 2010–11, Kessler won the Selke Award as the NHL's best defensive forward.

LEFT: When Kirk McLean got hot, he truly was "Fire on Ice."

CALLING THE SHOTS

Hockey is on the front of the sports pages 12 months a year in Vancouver. That makes the job of coaching the Canucks one of the most pressure-packed in the NHL. Only a few coaches have been able to succeed in this situation. Roger Neilson and Pat Quinn took the team to the Stanley Cup Finals, and Quinn later became the team's president.

Neilson was nicknamed "Rule Book Roger" because he could find clever ways to turn the game's rules to his advantage. The Canucks hired him as an assistant because he was known for teaching players how to think like winners. After Vancouver promoted him to head coach during the 1981–82 season, Neilson whipped the club into shape and got the Canucks to play winning hockey against the NHL's best teams.

Quinn was a top defenseman in the 1970s whose career ended early because of a broken ankle. After coaching the Philadelphia Flyers to the Stanley Cup in 1980, he took time off from hockey to earn a *law degree*. Quinn used his understanding of contracts to

Alain Vigneault checks the scoreboard as Daniel and Henrik Sedin take a rest on the bench.

become one of the game's most successful **executives**. In 1990, he moved behind the bench as coach and led the club to the Stanley Cup Finals three seasons later.

Another coach who enjoyed success in Vancouver was Marc Crawford. However, it was Alain Vigneault, the man who replaced Crawford, whom most fans pick as Vancouver's finest coach. Vigneault was a defenseman during his playing days with the St. Louis Blues. He believed that defense was the key to winning in the NHL.

Vigneault led the Canucks to six division titles in seven seasons. In his first year, 2006–07, Vancouver won 49 games, which was the most ever for the team at that time. Under Vigneault, the Canucks matched that win total in 2009–10, and then surpassed it in each of the next two seasons. In 2010–11, the Canucks had the most wins, the most goals, and the best defense in the league. That same season, Vigneault guided them to the Stanley Cup Finals.

ONE GREAT DAY

APRIL 30, 1994

A *generation* has passed since the deciding game of the 1994 Western Conference Quarterfinals between the Canucks and the Calgary Flames. Even so, Vancouver hockey fans still speak of it as if it happened yesterday. After falling behind, the Canucks had battled back to tie the series on overtime goals by Geoff Courtnall and Trevor Linden. But the Flames were a tough team. They were ready for Game 7.

The Flames went ahead 3–2 and held the lead late in the third period. The fans in Calgary stood and cheered as the minutes melted away. As hope was fading away for the Canucks, left wing Greg Adams found an opening and scored the game-tying goal. Adams netted only 13 goals during the year, but he had a great scoring touch in the playoffs.

After three periods, the game was tied. In the first overtime period, three Flames swooped in against defenseman Jyrki Lumme. Goalie Kirk McLean *anticipated* a shot by Theo Fleury. So did Lumme, who

Pavel Bure's goal-scoring made him front-page news in 1993–94.

rushed Fleury, leaving Robert Reichel undefended. Fleury then slid a perfect pass to Reichel, who had a wide-open goal. He cracked a shot toward the net from a few feet away, but McLean would not give in. He launched his body across the goal feet-first and stopped Reichel's shot with his toe!

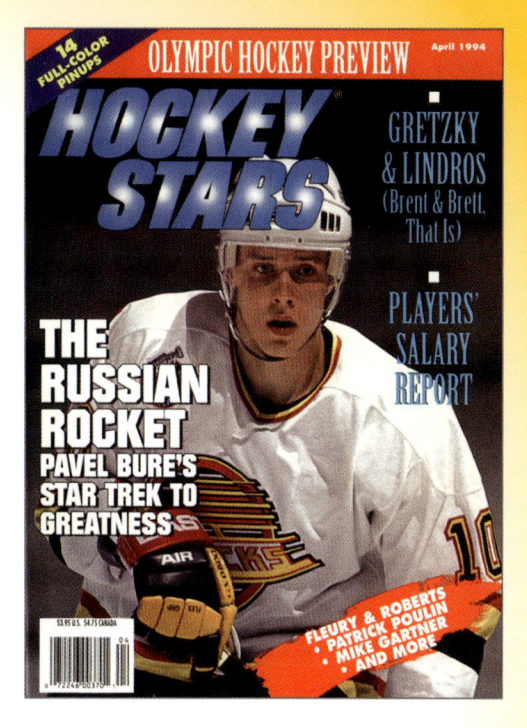

The teams played through the first overtime and began a second. A little over two minutes had ticked off the clock when Dave Babych skated up the ice with the puck. He spotted Jeff Brown in the open and fired a pass to him. As the Flames chased down Brown, Pavel Bure glided toward center ice. Brown lifted a pass right onto his stick.

The Russian Rocket blasted off. As he bore down on goalie Mike Vernon, Bure moved the puck to his backhand. The instant Vernon moved to stop this shot, Bure pulled the puck back and tucked it around the goalie's outstretched right pad for the winning goal. Bure threw his stick and gloves in the air and jumped into the arms of his teammates as they poured onto the ice.

LEGEND HAS IT

WHO WAS THE FIRST PLAYER TO TAKE A "STICK RIDE" AFTER SCORING A GOAL?

LEGEND HAS IT that Tiger Williams was. Williams did not want to leave Toronto when the Maple Leafs traded him to the Canucks in 1980. In no time, however, Williams realized what a fun place Vancouver was to live and play. During his first trip back to Toronto, the feisty forward scored against the Leafs and then hopped on his stick and rode it around the rink for a victory lap. Williams had the best year of his career with the Canucks, scoring 35 goals in all.

ABOVE: More than 30 years after his stick ride, Tiger Williams still loves to sign this photo. **RIGHT**: Wayne Maki was Vancouver's original number 11.

WILL THE CANUCKS LET ANOTHER PLAYER WEAR #11 AGAIN?

LEGEND HAS IT that they won't. Actually, for more than 20 years, Vancouver fans assumed that the number was retired, even though the jersey wasn't hanging from the rafters. Number 11 had belonged to Wayne Maki, an original member of the team who passed away in 1974. No player wore that jersey until Mark Messier joined the Canucks in 1997. The team allowed Messier to wear #11 (who had made it famous with two other teams). The Canucks promised Maki's widow that number 11 would be taken out of circulation when Messier was done, and it was.

HOW DID VANCOUVER FANS TELL THE SEDIN TWINS APART?

LEGEND HAS IT that their smiles were different. When Henrik and Daniel first joined the team, there was only one way to tell them apart when they were out of uniform: Henrik had a chipped front tooth. After he got it fixed, there was no easy way to tell. Of course, during games, Daniel (22) and Henrik (33) wore different numbers.

29

IT REALLY HAPPENED

Hockey teams have two bosses. The head coach trains the players and sets the *strategy* during games. The general manager assembles the **roster** and calls the shots off the ice. One of Vancouver's most famous general managers was Brian Burke. During the 1998–99 season, Burke made a bold decision. Henrik and Daniel Sedin were identical twins and two of the best young players in the world. Though both were guaranteed to go in the first round of the NHL draft, Burke wanted them to skate together for the Canucks.

Burke spent 10 weeks trying to figure out how he could pull off the impossible. The Canucks owned the third pick in the draft. Burke traded a future first-round pick and a player to get the fourth pick in the draft. Then he traded the fourth pick and two more draft choices for the first pick in the draft. Burke announced to reporters that no one would be leaving the draft with "both Sedins" except him.

Despite this boast, Burke was now worried that the Atlanta Thrashers would use the second pick in the draft to mess up his

Henrik Sedin was drafted by Vancouver just minutes after his brother Daniel in 1999.

plans. Fifteen minutes before the draft began, he traded his top pick to the Thrashers to move up to their spot. There was one condition to the deal: Atlanta promised not to take either Sedin brother.

Burke's wheeling and dealing paid off. He could barely contain himself as he called out Daniel's name with Vancouver's first pick. Burke then returned to the stage to call out Henrik's name with the next pick.

Both Henrik and Daniel would go on to win the Art Ross Trophy as the NHL scoring champion. Henrik was a **First-Team All-Star** in 2009–10 and again the following season. Daniel joined him on the First Team in 2010–11. Henrik also won the Hart Trophy as the NHL's **Most Valuable Player (MVP)** in 2009–10, when he broke Pavel Bure's team record with 112 points.

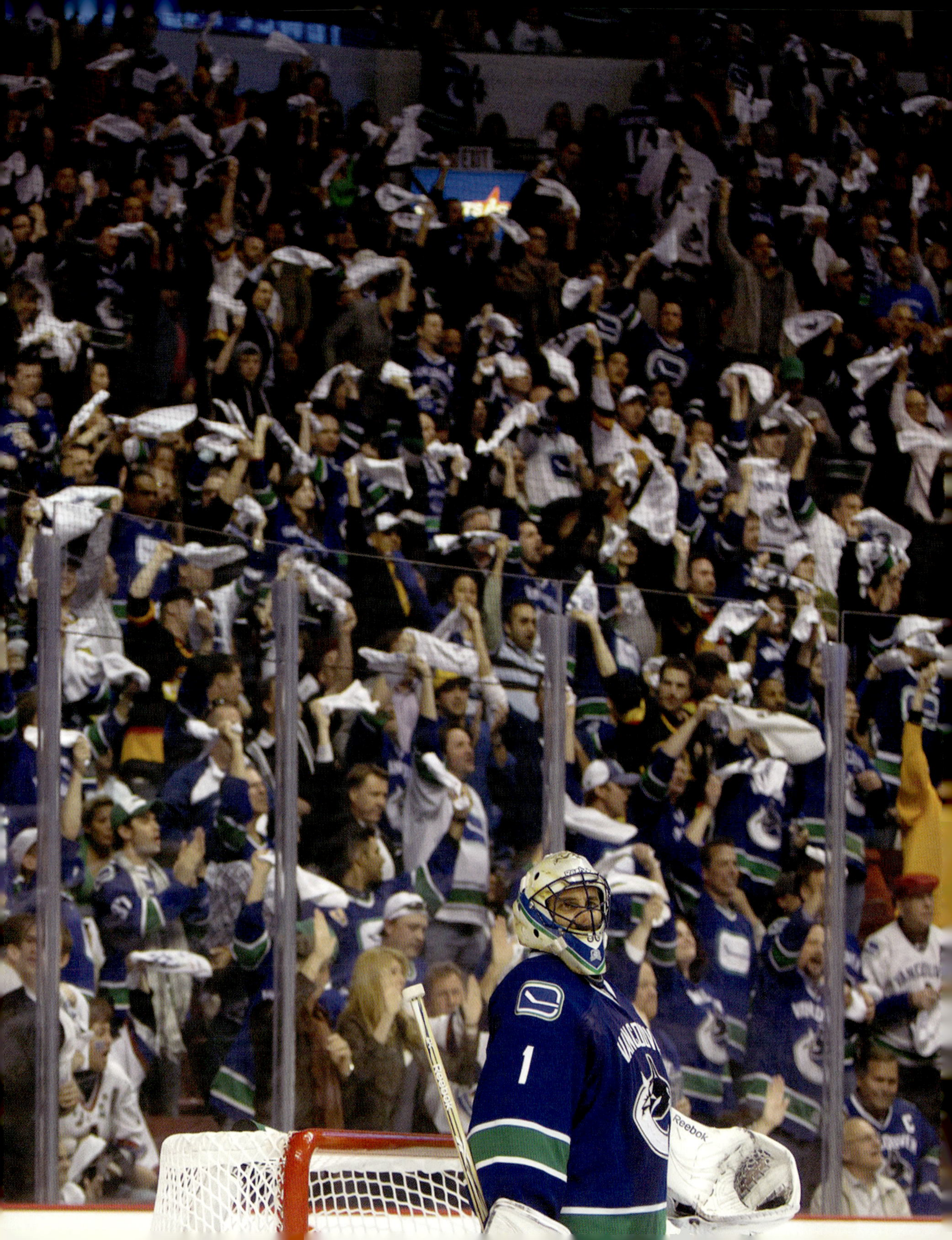
1
Reebok

TEAM SPIRIT

Vancouver fans eat, breathe, and sleep hockey. They also get very, very loud during home games. That gives the Canucks a big advantage. Canucks fans became part of hockey lore in 1982. During a frustrating playoff loss in Chicago to the Blackhawks, coach Roger Neilson waved a white towel after one of several poor calls by the referee. He meant it as an insult. When other players on the bench did the same, Neilson was thrown out of the game.

When the series moved back to Vancouver, the players were amazed to see an ocean of twirling white towels. They realized what a strong bond they had created with their fans. The Canucks won the next three games to upset Chicago and make it to the Stanley Cup Finals. More than 30 years later, Canucks fans still use "Towel Power" whenever their team needs it.

LEFT: Roberto Luongo soaks up a little "Towel Power."
ABOVE: Pat Quinn graces the cover of this game program from the team's early years.

TIMELINE

The hockey season is played from October through June. That means each season takes place at the end of one year and the beginning of the next. In this timeline, the accomplishments of the Canucks are shown by season.

1974–75
Vancouver has its first winning season.

1982–83
Darcy Rota has the Canucks' first 40-goal season.

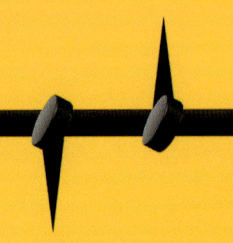

1970–71
The Canucks play their first NHL season.

1981–82
The team reaches the Stanley Cup Finals for the first time.

1992–93
Pavel Bure has the team's first 100-point season.

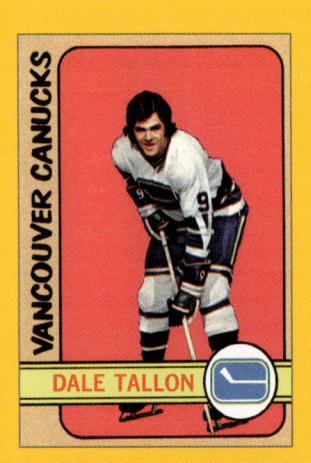

Dale Tallon was one of the team's first stars.

Stan Smyl captained the 1981–82 team

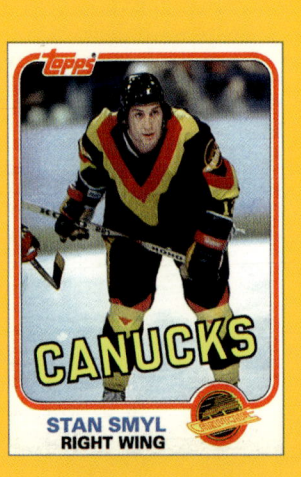

Shawn Antoski flies toward the goal in the 1994 playoffs.

1993-94
The Canucks reach the Stanley Cup Finals for the second time.

2002-03
Markus Naslund scores 12 game-winning goals.

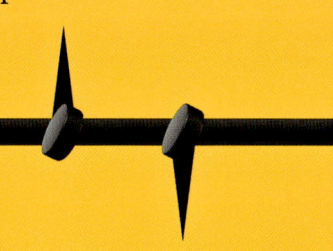

2000-01
Henrik and Daniel Sedin join the club.

2010-11
The team plays in the Stanley Cup Finals for the third time.

2012-13
Henrik Sedin becomes the team's all-time leader in points.

The Canucks celebrate their third trip to the finals.

FUN FACTS

FIRST AND LAST

Defenseman Barry Wilkins scored the first goal in team history, against the Los Angeles Kings. In 1974, when he was traded to the Pittsburgh Penguins, Wilkins was the last Canuck left from the team's 1970 expansion draft.

THE BREAKAWAY KID

Pavel Bure was always being pulled down from behind on breakaways with the Canucks. As a result, he retired as the league's all-time leader in **penalty shots**. In 1997–98, Bure set a record when he scored on penalty shots three times in the same season.

ONE FOR THE BOOKS

The first great victory in Canucks history came in February of 1971, when they defeated the champion Boston Bruins, 5–4. The hero for Vancouver was Rosie Paiement, who outplayed the great Bobby Orr. He scored three goals, including the game-winner with less than a minute to play.

TAYLOR MADE

Each year, the Canucks give the Cyclone Taylor Award to the team MVP. Fred Taylor was the star of the 1915 Vancouver Millionaires, who won the Stanley Cup. Markus Naslund won the award a record five times.

PASSING FANCY

In a 1984 game in Pittsburgh against the Penguins, Patrik Sundstrom set up six goals and scored one himself in a 9–5 victory. His six assists tied an NHL record for a player in a road game, and his seven points set a new team record.

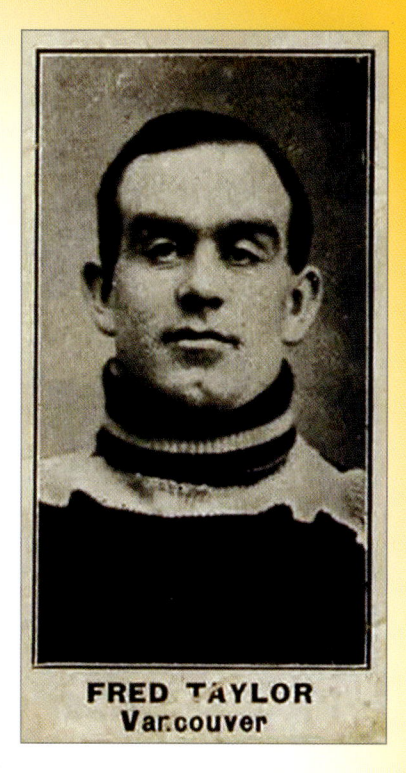

TARGET PRACTICE

During the 1994 playoffs, goalie Kirk McLean faced a whopping 820 shots in 24 games. No one before or since has topped 800 in a postseason.

ROAD WARRIORS

In the early part of 2010, the Canucks' home ice was used for the *Olympics*. As a result, the team was forced to play 14 away games in a row. It was the longest "road trip" in NHL history.

ABOVE: Fred "Cyclone" Taylor

TALKING HOCKEY

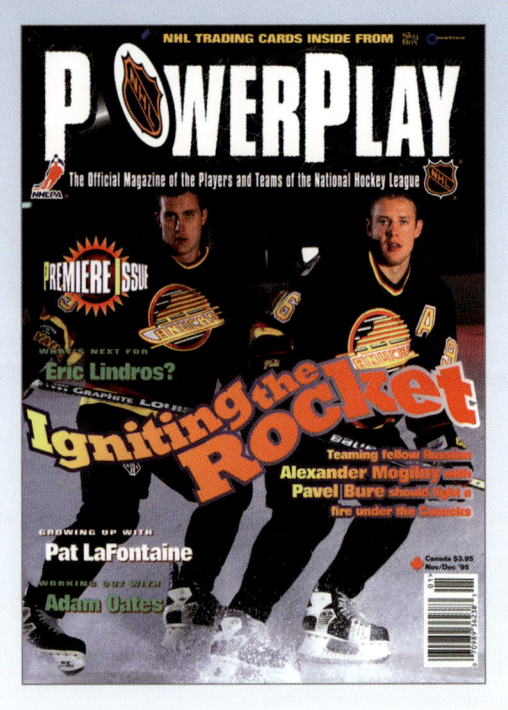

"Getting lucky is just part of the game."
▶ **KIRK McLEAN,** *on making some of his greatest saves*

"You've got to be aware of him when he's on the ice, but you've got to make sure not to get caught up in chasing him all over. That's what he wants."
▶ **ALEXANDER MOGILNY,** *on the clever way linemate Pavel Bure used his speed*

"Maybe we didn't draft the best player in the league when we got 'Kurt' … but we certainly drafted the best captain."
▶ **HAL LAYCOE,** *on Orland Kurtenbach*

"Skating is the strong part of my game. I was never considered a scorer, even in Sweden."
▶ **THOMAS GRADIN,** *on how he blossomed after coming to the NHL*

38

"I remember expecting to play on different teams, actually. All the talk before the draft was that there was no way we would be able to play together, so we were ready to be apart."

▶ **DANIEL SEDIN,** *on being drafted by the Canucks with Henrik*

"In everything we do, whether it's tennis or golf or hockey, we're competitive. I think it's a good thing because we push each other to do better."

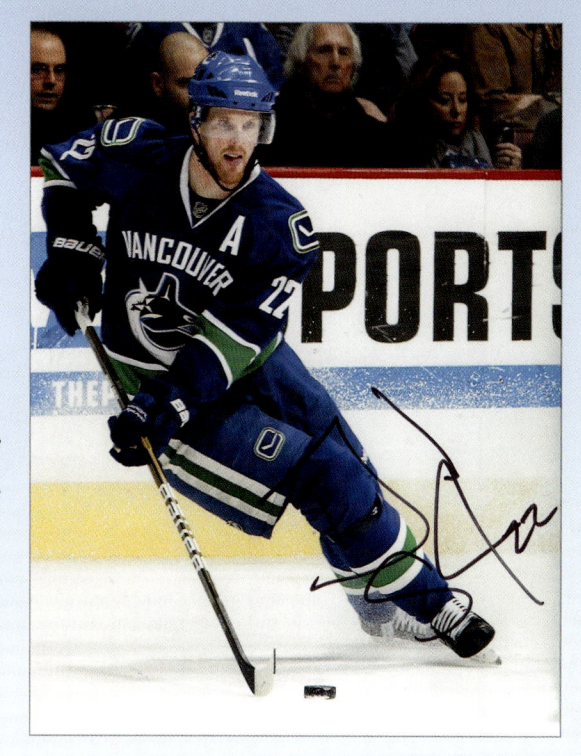

▶ **HENRIK SEDIN,** *on his relationship with Daniel*

"A lot of people looked at it and said, 'Wow, that's really young to be a captain.' But for me it was pretty natural. Everybody is made differently … and for me it was pretty natural."

▶ **TREVOR LINDEN,** *on being named team captain at the age of 21*

LEFT: Alexander Mogilny and Pavel Bure share the cover of a hockey magazine. The two Russian stars were teammates in Vancouver for three seasons. **ABOVE**: Daniel Sedin

GREAT DEBATES

People who root for the Canucks love to compare their favorite moments, teams, and players. Some debates have been going on for years! How would you settle these classic hockey arguments?

VANCOUVER'S ALL-TIME GREATEST LINE WAS THE WESTERN EXPRESS LINE...

... because it perfectly combined the talents of three different players. Markus Naslund (**LEFT**) was a first-rate scorer, Todd Bertuzzi was big and tough, and Brendan Morrison was one of the smartest players in the NHL. In 2002–03, each of the three had the best season of his career—a rare feat for three players on the same line. They scored 119 goals and had 272 points that year.

NO WAY. THE IKEA LINE WAS THE GREATEST...

... because it teamed up Naslund with two better players: Henrik and Daniel Sedin. The line got its name from the department store that started in Sweden; all three players were from that country. In 2006–07, the IKEA Line scored 70 goals and had 225 points. These numbers came in a year when the Canucks were focused on defense. Naslund and the Sedins also helped Vancouver win 49 games—the most in team history at that time.

ROBERTO LUONGO WAS THE CANUCKS' BEST GOALIE ...

… because he covered the net better than any goalie in team history. Luongo used his pads and stick to deflect shots, and no one was better at stealing goals with his glove. Also, he never seemed to get tired; he was good for 70 or more games a year. Luongo was a Second-Team All-Star in 2004 and 2007, and had the NHL's lowest goals-against average in 2010–11. In 2006–07—his first season in Vancouver—Luongo won 47 games and was a finalist for the Hart Trophy as league MVP.

ARE YOU KIDDING? KIRK McLEAN WILL ALWAYS BE VANCOUVER'S ALL-TIME BEST ...

… because when a brilliant save was needed, no one was better than "Captain Kirk." He may not have been as big or as quick as Luongo, but McLean (**RIGHT**) won 24 games during the 1993–94 playoffs and stopped a record number of shots. That spring, the Canucks made it all the way to the Stanley Cup Finals. Without McLean, they wouldn't have survived the opening round.

FOR THE RECORD

The great Canucks teams and players have left their marks on the record books. These are the "best of the best" …

Trevor Linden

Roberto Luongo

CANUCKS AWARD WINNERS

ART ROSS TROPHY
TOP SCORER

Henrik Sedin	2009–10
Daniel Sedin	2010–11

FRANK J. SELKE TROPHY
TOP DEFENSIVE FORWARD

Ryan Kesler	2010–11

HART MEMORIAL TROPHY
MOST VALUABLE PLAYER

Henrik Sedin	2009–10

JACK ADAMS AWARD
COACH OF THE YEAR

Pat Quinn	1991–92
Alain Vigneault	2006–07

KING CLANCY MEMORIAL TROPHY
ANNUAL HUMANITARIAN AWARD

Trevor Linden	1996–97

LESTER B. PEARSON AWARD
MOST OUTSTANDING PLAYER

Markus Naslund	2002–03

TED LINDSAY AWARD
MOST OUTSTANDING PLAYER

Markus Naslund	2002–03*
Daniel Sedin	2010–11

WILLIAM JENNINGS TROPHY
GOALTENDER WITH FEWEST GOALS ALLOWED

Roberto Luongo & Cory Schneider	2010–11

* The Ted Lindsay Award was known as the Lester B. Pearson Award until 2010 when the NHL changed the name.

42

CANUCKS ACHIEVEMENTS

ACHIEVEMENT	YEAR
Smythe Division Champions	1974–75
Smythe Division Champions	1981–82
Campbell Conference Champions	1981–82
Smythe Division Champions	1991–92
Smythe Division Champions	1992–93
Western Conference Champions	1993–94
Northwest Division Champions	2003–04
Northwest Division Champions	2006–07
Northwest Division Champions	2008–09
Northwest Division Champions	2009–10
Northwest Division Champions	2010–11
Western Conference Champions	2010–11
Northwest Division Champions	2011–12
Northwest Division Champions	2012–13

Todd Bertuzzi was a star for the 2003–04 champs.

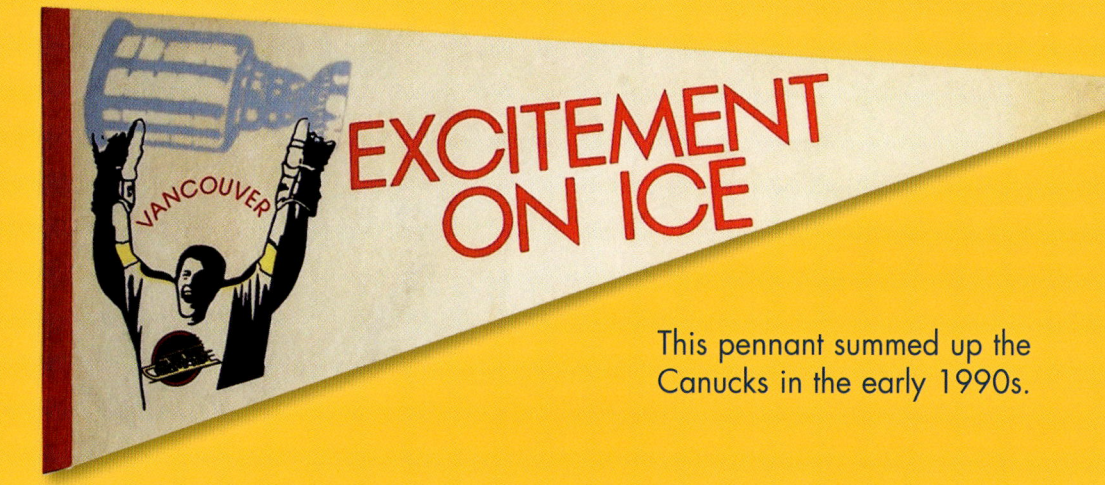

This pennant summed up the Canucks in the early 1990s.

PINPOINTS

The history of a hockey team is made up of many smaller stories. These stories take place all over the map—not just in the city a team calls "home." Match the pushpins on these maps to the **TEAM FACTS**, and you will begin to see the story of the Canucks unfold!

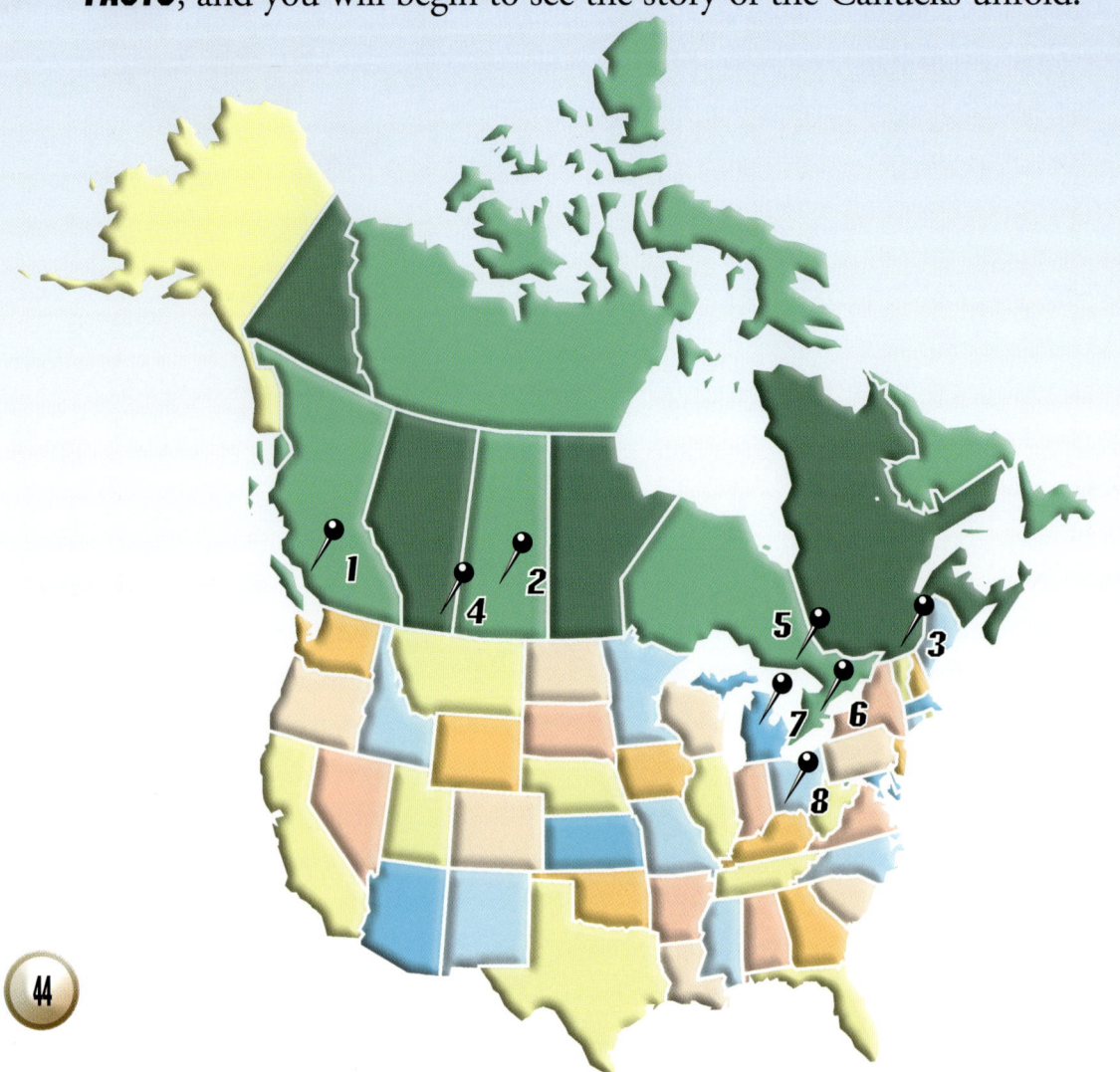

44

TEAM FACTS

1 Vancouver, British Columbia—*The Canucks have played here since 1970.*
2 Cudworth, Saskatchewan—*Orland Kurtenbach was born here.*
3 Montreal, Quebec—*Roberto Luongo was born here.*
4 Medicine Hat, Alberta—*Trevor Linden was born here.*
5 Sudbury, Ontario—*Todd Bertuzzi was born here.*
6 Hamilton, Ontario—*Pat Quinn was born here.*
7 Livonia, Michigan—*Ryan Kesler was born here.*
8 Cincinnati, Ohio—*Curt Fraser was born here.*
9 Örnsköldsvik, Sweden—*Henrik & Daniel Sedin were born here.*
10 Moscow, Russia—*Pavel Bure was born here.*
11 Most, Czech Republic—*Ivan Hlinka was born here.*
12 Turku, Finland—*Sami Salo was born here.*

Orland Kurtenbach

GLOSSARY

HOCKEY WORDS
VOCABULARY WORDS

ALL-STAR GAME—The annual game that features the best players from the NHL.

ANTICIPATED—Expected something to happen before it did.

ASSISTS—Passes that lead to a goal.

CONFERENCE—A large group of teams. There are two conferences in the NHL, and each season each conference sends a team to the Stanley Cup Finals.

DIVERSE—Varied or different.

DIVISION—A small group of teams in a conference. Each NHL conference has three divisions.

EXECUTIVES—People who make important decisions for a company.

EXPANSION DRAFT—A meeting at which teams new to a league get to select players from teams already in the league.

FIRST-TEAM ALL-STAR—The annual award that recognizes the best NHL player at each position.

GENERATION—A period of years roughly equal to the time it takes for a person to be born, grow up, and have children.

HALL OF FAME—The museum in Toronto, Canada, where hockey's best players are honored. A player voted into the Hall of Fame is sometimes called a "Hall of Famer."

LAW DEGREE—The diploma earned by someone after finishing law school.

LINE—The trio made up by a left wing, center, and right wing.

LOGO—A symbol or design that represents a company or team.

MINOR LEAGUES—All the professional leagues that operate below the NHL.

MOST VALUABLE PLAYER (MVP)—The award given each year to the league's best player; also given to the best player in the playoffs and All-Star Game.

NATIONAL BASKETBALL ASSOCIATION (NBA)—The professional league that has been operating since 1946.

NATIONAL HOCKEY LEAGUE (NHL)—The professional league that has been operating since 1917.

OLYMPICS—An international summer or winter sports competition held every four years.

OVERTIME—An extra period played when a game is tied after three periods. In the NHL playoffs, teams continue to play overtime periods until a goal is scored.

PENALTY SHOTS—Shots awarded to a player when an obvious scoring opportunity is stopped by an illegal play.

PLAYOFFS—The games played after the season to determine the league champion.

POSTSEASON—Another term for playoffs.

PROVINCE—A region of Canada, somewhat similar to a state.

ROSTER—The list of players on a team.

STANLEY CUP—The trophy presented to the NHL champion. The first Stanley Cup was awarded in 1893.

STANLEY CUP FINALS—The final playoff series that determines the winner of the Stanley Cup.

STRATEGY—A plan or method for succeeding.

TELECOMMUNICATIONS—Technology that deals with the phone.

WRIST SHOTS—Shots taken by "flicking" the puck with a quick turn of the wrists.

LINE CHANGE

TEAM SPIRIT introduces a great way to stay up to date with your team! Visit our **LINE CHANGE** link and get connected to the latest and greatest updates. **LINE CHANGE** serves as a young reader's ticket to an exclusive web page—with more stories, fun facts, team records, and photos of the Canucks. Content is updated during and after each season. The **LINE CHANGE** feature also enables readers to send comments and letters to the author! Log onto:

www.norwoodhousepress.com/library.aspx

and click on the tab: **TEAM SPIRIT** to access **LINE CHANGE**.

Read all the books in the series to learn more about professional sports. For a complete listing of the baseball, basketball, football, and hockey teams in the **TEAM SPIRIT** series, visit our website at:

www.norwoodhousepress.com/library.aspx

ON THE ROAD

VANCOUVER CANUCKS
800 Griffiths Way
Vancouver, British Columbia, Canada V6B 6G1
(604) 899-4600
http://canucks.nhl.com

HOCKEY HALL OF FAME
Brookfield Place
30 Yonge Street
Toronto, Ontario, Canada M5E 1X8
(416) 360-7765
http://www.hhof.com

ON THE BOOKSHELF

To learn more about the sport of hockey, look for these books at your library or bookstore:

- Cameron, Steve. *Hockey Hall of Fame Treasures.* Richmond Hill, Ontario, Canada: Firefly Books, 2011.
- Keltie, Thomas. *Inside Hockey! The legends, facts, and feats that made the game.* Toronto, Ontario, Canada: Maple Tree Press, 2008.
- Romanuk, Paul. *Scholastic Canada Book of Hockey Lists.* Markham, Ontario, Canada: Scholastic Canada, 2007.

INDEX

PAGE NUMBERS IN **BOLD** REFER TO ILLUSTRATIONS.

Adams, Greg	26	McLean, Kirk	10, 17, 18, 22, 22, 26, 27, 37, 38, 41, **41**
Adams, Jack	6, **6**	Messier, Mark	29
Antoski, Shawn	**35**	Mogilny, Alexander	38, **38**
Bertuzzi, Todd	10, 40, **43**, 45	Morrison, Brendan	10, 40
Babych, Dave	27	Naslund, Markus	10, 13, 23, 35, 37, 40, **40**, 42
Bieksa, Kevin	19	Neale, Harry	16
Boldirev, Ivan	16	Neilson, Roger	16, 24, 33
Boudrias, Andre	9, **15**, 20	Ohlund, Mattias	10
Brodeur, Richard	9, 16	Orr, Bobby	36
Brown, Jeff	18, 27	Paiement, Rosie	36
Bure, Pavel	10, **10**, 17, 18, 22, 27, **27**, 31, 34, 36, 38, **38**, 45	Poile, Bud	7
Burke, Brian	30, 31	Quinn, Pat	9, **9**, 10, 17, 24, **33**, 42, 45
Burrows, Alex	**4**, 10, 11, 19	Reichel, Robert	27
Courtnall, Geoff	17, **17**, 26	Rota, Darcy	34
Crawford, Marc	25	Salo, Sami	10, 45
Doak, Gary	7	Schneider, Cory	42
Fleury, Theo	26, 27	Sedin, Daniel	11, **11**, 19, 23, **25**, 29, 30, 31, 35, 39, **39**, 40, 42, 45
Gradin, Thomas	9, 16, 21, **21**, 38		
Guevremont, Jocelyn	9	Sedin, Henrik	11, **11**, 19, 23, **25**, 29, 30, 31, **31**, 35, 39, 40, 42, 45
Hamhuis, Dan	10, **11**		
Hlinka, Ivan	16, 45		
Kesler, Ryan	**4**, 10, 11, 19, 23, 42, 45	Smyl, Stan	9, 13, 16, **16**, 21, 34
Kurtenbach, Orland	**8**, 9, 20, 38, 45, **45**	Snepts, Harold	16, **16**
		Sundstrom, Patrik	9, 21, 22, 37
Laycoe, Hall	7, 38	Tallon, Dale	9, **34**
Lever, Don	9	Tanti, Tony	9
Linden, Trevor	10, 13, 17, 18, **18**, 22, 26, 39, 42, **42**, 45	Taylor, Fred "Cyclone"	6, 37, **37**
		Vernon, Mike	27
Lumme, Jyrki	26	Vigneault, Alain	25, **25**, 42
Luongo, Roberto	10, **14**, 18, 19, **19**, **32**, 41, 42, **42**, 45	Wilkins, Barry	36
		Williams, Tiger	16, 28, **28**
Maki, Wayne	29, **29**		

THE TEAM

MARK STEWART has written over 200 books for kids—and more than a dozen books on hockey, including a history of the Stanley Cup and an authorized biography of goalie Martin Brodeur. He grew up in New York City during the 1960s rooting for the Rangers, but has gotten to know a couple of New Jersey Devils, so he roots for a shootout when these teams play each other. Mark comes from a family of writers. His grandfather was Sunday Editor of *The New York Times,* and his mother was Articles Editor of *Ladies' Home Journal* and *McCall's*. Mark has profiled hundreds of athletes over the past 25 years. He has also written several books about his native New York and New Jersey, his home today. Mark is a graduate of Duke University, with a degree in history. He lives and works in a home overlooking Sandy Hook, New Jersey. You can contact Mark through the Norwood House Press website.

DENIS GIBBONS is a writer and editor with *The Hockey News* and a former newsletter editor of the Toronto-based Society for International Hockey Research (SIHR). He was a contributing writer to the publication *Kings of the Ice: A History of World Hockey* and has worked as chief hockey researcher at five Winter Olympics for the ABC, CBS, and NBC television networks. Denis also has worked as a researcher for the FOX Sports Network during the Stanley Cup playoffs. He resides in Burlington, Ontario, Canada with his wife Chris.